Bottoms UP

Allie Alexander & Tripp Elliot

By: Allie Alexander

ISBN:0692324364

ISBN-13:978-0692324363

By: Allie Alexander

Table of Contents

Intro:

So, after being married for 8 years, and together for eleven, it was time to have "The Talk" with my husband. You know the one: "Honey, I am completely satisfied with our sex life, but…" I wanted a little more romance, a little more danger, something to add spice to the usual, "You wanna?" and "Yeah, I guess," Tuesday night ritual. We opened a bottle of wine, I lit some candles, and I told him we should write down some things that we wanted from each other sexually. He agreed and we got to work. I had already planned out what I was going to write:

- Maybe we could look into tying you up instead of me all of the time?
- Let's look into each other's eyes as we climax and really find a deeper intimacy level.
- What if I go to a bar and you walk in and hit on me like we didn't know each other?
- What are your thoughts on role-playing?

- What if I danced for you, you know, like a stripper?
- Will you buy me some lingerie that you pick out?
- Would you consider a little S&M?
- Let's look online at a sex-toy shop and buy all new toys to play with!

<u>His list:</u>

a) Threesome
b) Anal

It's not like I couldn't have guessed. What guy doesn't want a threesome or anal, or a threesome that involves anal? The problem was how was I going to make this happen? Sex with a third partner seemed a lot harder to pull off than anal. I have the equipment for anal in my back pocket, so-to-speak. The problem was, that back door became permanently locked the first time we tried that position. He agreed to try at least three of my requests if I agreed to try one of his. Out of the two, anal was my preference, but not the 'painful, I can't really handle it and never want to try it again' part of anal sex. I was hoping to discover the 'this is the hottest thing we have ever done' aspect of anal, mixed with 'Omg, I think this feels great' part if that was possible for me. It was time to ask for help.

If there has ever been a reason to call the Rainbow Hotline, I would say that a gay man giving advice on how to have anal sex should be at the top of the priority list for straight women emergencies. I placed my 911 to my best friend, Tripp, to see what he could do to help a sister out. Tripp answered on the first ring and, before he could even say hello, I blurted everything into the phone:

"TRIPP!! I NEED YOU! Dylan and I wrote down things that we wanted sexually from each other and he wants a threesome or anal and a threesome is not in the cards so anal it is but it hurts too much and I just can't so I need you to teach me how to get my husband's huge square peg package into my tiny round hole."

There was a brief pause before Tripp answered:

"Allie – um, do you remember how my phone blue-tooth's to my car so that I can hear you through my speakers, and more importantly, do you remember this was the day my mother and I were driving around looking for a new condo for her?"

"Oh – yeah, right…that's today? Mrs. Elliot, how are you?"

Needless to say, Tripp and I decided to meet later for cocktails.

Happy Hour

It took one and a half dirty martinis and three orders of fried appetizers to convince me there would be a day I could look Tripp's mother in the eye again. Or at least in the vicinity of her chin. Once the vodka and olive brine started loosening me up, I decided it was time to ask my questions.

"So, Tripp, can you help me?"

After calling the extremely attractive bartender over, because he, too, was a "bottom," my cheerleaders began coaching me to the finish line – or coaching me on how to get my husband to finish inside the very fine line, so to speak.

Now that one night of cocktails has made me an anal expert, I can't wait to share my newfound knowledge with all of you. While I can't meet everyone out for martinis, I can certainly pour myself one and field your questions here. Just one moment please...

Here we go: Dirty, extra dry, and shaken like a rag doll. I wish this was an "I like my martinis like I like my men" joke, but extra dry and shaken like a rag doll doesn't sound appealing. Dirty will work though...

I'm ready, ladies, ask away:

Q1: "What Do I Get Out of It?"

At the end of the day, anal is probably not going to give you the biggest orgasm you have ever had. Then why do so many gay men do it? You see they were blessed with a prostate, which provides mind-blowing orgasms. Their prostate is located about three inches up inside the anal cavity.

We, on the other hand, have nada in there that creates an orgasm. If your man enters you from behind, or in the behind I should say, it is best to have a front door plan so that something, or someone, is stimulating you there if you want to ride those waves of pleasure that he is about to embark upon. So, why would we do it?

1st – This is something exciting you are doing for your partner. If you ask him to have a romantic night with you, to go down on you a lot longer than he actually wants to, or to say loving words in your ear during intercourse, these are sexual desires you are expressing. He has in turn expressed a desire by telling you he wants anal sex. So, the experience is a gift you are giving your partner.

<u>2nd</u> – All is not lost in your orgasm world if entry to the backdoor is successful. This is an experience that will drive your lover crazy, and one that will have an effect on your libido. His heightened state of ecstasy will, in turn, heighten your arousal and your ability to orgasm with a vibrator, or his or your fingers can provide overwhelming sensations that will make you want another night of anal.

<u>3rd</u> – This experience will bring you closer to your partner in many ways. There are plenty of preparations to take care of to make the anal sex more pleasurable for you, and your husband can be a part of them. You will probably notice a change in his mood as you guys discuss, flirt, and ultimately look forward to the time when this fantasy is fulfilled. "Happy Husband, Happy Home" isn't the saying, but "Happy Husband, Awesome Sex Life" is probably cross stitched above a fireplace somewhere.

Tripp's Tips

What do you get out of it? Honey, anything you want! He will do the dishes, bring you breakfast in bed, and those new shoes you've been wanting? All yours. You are about to give him an AMAZING orgasm and an experience he has been fantasizing about since the day he met you! Go get it, girl! And by the way, don't forget, there are thousands of nerve endings inside your rectum that are just waiting to be stimulated for your own pleasure!

Q2: "It Hurts"

We'll get to that. We have other ground to cover first…

Q3: "Should I Lie On My Stomach or My Back? How Flexible Do I Have to Be?"

You really do like to jump ahead, don't you? That is up and coming as well, but a nice segue into the communication piece. Communication is a big deal – anal is apparently important to him sexually and you have some concerns about this act. Before the big night, or afternoon, or morning – I don't really know when you have sex – so, let's say before the big moment arrives, a conversation is needed. What if his fantasy involves you bent over the hood of his car at the drive-in? For that you are going to have to tell him it is illegal and he has the potential to get plenty of what he is looking for if you guys are arrested. You can't promise he will be in the position he wants, but hey, anal is anal, right?

An open line of communication will be key for this activity. He needs to let you know what he is looking for, and you need to tell him some of the things you will need to seal the deal. You might even suggest he reads this book so that he knows everything you are doing to make this fantasy happen! As for comfortable positions, we will cover that shortly in our "Journey To The Center

Of You" guidebook.

Tripp's Tips:

Talk about this while you are in the act! Imagine your husband in the middle of your lovemaking when you whisper in his ear, "Soon baby, I am going to let you have what you want. I WANT anal." Girl, he will finish so fast you won't have to worry about having it that night. Communication is a great and healthy tool, but a little dirty talk is even better.

Q4: "How Can I Make It Exciting Before We Actually Do It?"

To be perfectly cliché, Rome wasn't built in a day. This means that you have plenty of time for teasers to really drive your partner crazy. Maybe watch some anal porn with him one night and let him know that his turn is very soon. Send him a link to a sex toy site and ask him to pick out a couple of things for your anal extravaganza. A few sexy texts saying that you are looking forward to anal with him might bring him home early from work one day for a little fun!

My husband and I created a code word for anal and we had fun talking about it in the open. Remember when I said Rome wasn't built in a day? Well that's what I told him when he asked me exactly when this was going to happen. And there it was: Anal sex was forever dubbed, "Romeing." Alex began asking me if we could visit Rome soon, Rome must be nice this time of year, he's heard that Rome is the most beautiful city in the world. We thought we were pretty clever until our oldest told my in-laws that she heard her daddy on the phone talking about a vacation to Rome and she didn't think that we were taking her or her siblings with us. Alex's mother starting asking questions about our upcoming trip to the City of Fountains. To be specific, she asked me when exactly we were going to Rome, how long we would be in Rome, and my favorite:

"My son has always wanted to go to Rome!"

Tell me something I don't know.

Tripp's Tips:

This is YOUR chance to get into this. You can sext with your partner, or send a sexy e-mail. Be the hot diva that you are and drive that man crazy! My best tip for this is double check your recipient before you hit send...

If you are not comfortable with electronic messages, go and buy a card and leave it on his pillow, next to his morning coffee, in his briefcase, wherever he will see it. Let him know what you are thinking, feeling, wanting. Own your sexuality, girlfriend!

Q5: "Um, Well, I Don't Want Him to See Anything That Might Be in There, If You Know What I Mean?"

Ladies, let's just get this part out of the way. Your sphincter has two roles at this point: To help you eliminate waste from your body and to provide your boyfriend, friend with pretty terrific benefits, fiancé, husband, whomever, with a night he has been fantasizing about forever. Let's see how we can keep these roles separate for your big night.

If this is something that you have planned, one easy way not to excrete waste is to not have any. In other words, limit your food intake before the big show. In no way am I suggesting unhealthy eating, or not eating, habits. Why bother? You already have your man – no need to buy the book, "Skinny Bitch" and starve yourself into a hot outfit. [Side note: There is every reason to buy that book. It is a really good guide to healthy living and eating, but it made the diatribe funny so…].

Once you have eliminated waste close enough to the time of the big backdoor bang, you can simply stop eating for a couple hours. No food, no waste, no excrement. [Side note 2: Do not, under any circumstances, practice unhealthy consumption techniques. Girl, if you are hungry, eat. However, if you have had your meal and it has digested and left the building, then enjoy your man for a couple hours to make sure you are running on empty and then you might feel more comfortable with the experience.]

The best way to make sure you excrete in a timeline you want is an enema or douche. You can pick one up at a drugstore and flush away your fears. You will need at least 20 to 30 minutes after you insert an enema for what's inside to travel outside. I'd go ahead and add another ten minutes for good measure, personally. After that, your engine is clean and will run smoothly for the next few miles.

Tripp's Tips:

For the professionals, there is an anal douche attachment for your shower. If you and your partner decide to engage in this activity on a regular basis, this is an integral investment to personal hygiene for continuous anal sex.

Allie's first encounter with one was at my house. She stayed the night and after showering the next morning, texted me this while I was at work:

"Is the silver cylindrical attachment in your shower what I think it is?"

My response?

"Well don't use it as a Waterpik."

In addition, if you want to avoid this question at your house, purchase a normal hand-held shower attachment that you can switch out with your douche attachment.

Q6: "What About Being Safe? Will a Condom Make it Hurt More?"

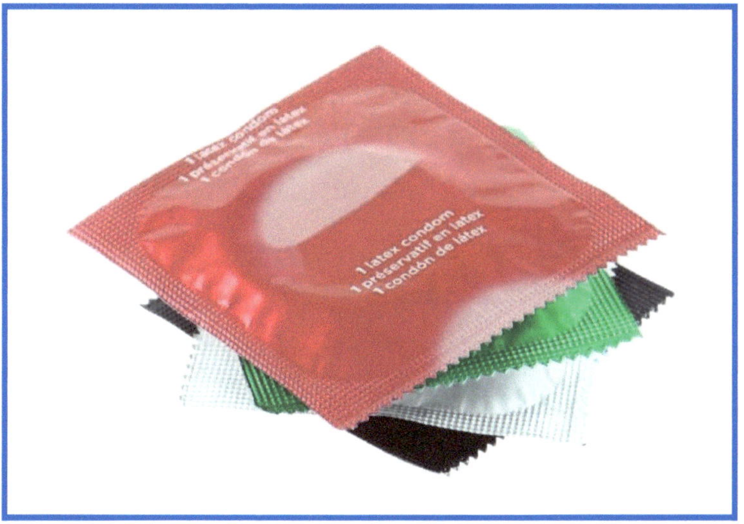

If you have been married, or together, for some time, you are both faithful and your tests have come back clean, then you have the means to make a safe decision about whether or not you would like to use this precaution. However, anything short of that and the best advice any gay, straight, bi, tri, whatever they are guy or girl can give you is: USE A CONDOM. You are already going to experience some discomfort for your first time and a condom is not going to make or break you, unless you don't use one and you end up with a sexually transmitted disease. That will break a lot of things. All tongue-in-cheek aside, safety first is the only option here.

Tripp's Tips:

If you want advice from a gay guy, then my best advice is that you take Allie's answer very seriously. If you are NOT in a fully committed and safe relationship, then take the steps necessary to protect both of you, and have a worry-free, HOT night of anal! Also, if you are using toys and decide to share, always put a condom on your shared sex toys to maintain safe hygiene levels.

Q7: "Can We Get Back to the Part Where It Might Hurt?"

Of course we can – you have several options to help alleviate the initial discomfort you might feel. Some of them are actually quite fun!

1) Relax. If you are stressed and/or worried about this, you will clench your muscles and cause your anus to tighten even more. You could start with taking a bubble bath together and enjoy some intimate moments in the water. Perhaps your partner can give you a massage to loosen your muscles and relax your whole body. After a massage is the perfect time for oral sex. This way, you are relaxed and extremely aroused. After a bath, and/or a massage, plus a few orgasms, it might be time to attempt anal sex! Don't worry if you decide you are not ready yet - he's been ready since the first time you had sex. A few more minutes or an extra night without it won't hurt him.

2) Work up to this epic event. For this exercise you will need two or three different sized vibrators or anal dildos, and of course, every anus' best friend – lube. You can do this over a

few nights, or “pack it all in” in one night. Have him start with his finger in order to begin the process of loosening this very tight space. A little lube and one of his digits and you can get a feel for how tight you really are. If a finger is painful, then you might need to work up to the next step, which is the thinnest vibrator. If his finger slides right in, then have him grab the lube and get the first vibrator ready. As he is using the first vibrator, grab a different vibrator and stimulate yourself externally. This will cause a distraction if you feel a pinch while the anal vibrator slides in, and it will enhance the experience for you by creating pleasure when you thought there might be pain. And let’s face it, this will drive your lover wild to see you masturbating while he is playing out back. Keep working up to thicker and longer devices so that you loosen the muscles in your anal canal.

Tripp's Tips:

If you need to practice with toys a few nights in a row, make sure you do so over three or more consecutive days. You don't want to wait a week after successfully inserting the thinnest vibrator as your muscles will return to their previous size and you will have to start over. If you can't work up to anal with your partner's penis in one night, plan a few nights and mornings in succession.

3) Lube is the key – the better the lube, the more chances you have of full insertion. Make sure that the lube you are using works with the materials his condom is made of (if you are using one). You don't want the condom's physical properties to break down and cause a safety issue with STD's. With that said, have your partner use lube on the outside of your anus, and then insert lube into you with his finger or a vibrator before you begin. Next, have him put it on himself to help glide easily into your anal canal.

Tripp's Tips:

To help with relaxing the nerves, there is a product called Anal-Eaze. If your lover puts a small amount inside of you a few minutes before anal intercourse, you will be able to tolerate his tool. HOWEVER, it can also numb his member so that it makes it difficult for him to finish! I suggest he wear a condom if you are using Anal-Eaze so that he does not feel the effects of the nerve-numbing agent.

As for other lubes, it depends on how slick and long lasting you prefer. Silicone lubes are your top choice for a long-lasting lubricant and easy glide-in (especially good for really tight places), but they are more likely to stain your sheets. You can also choose a water-based lube, but in many cases you will find they don't last long enough. However, they are much nicer on your linens! Bottom line, use a silicone lube the first few times and just put a towel down on the sheets.

4) *Distractions* – We already covered masturbating; can you imagine a better distraction? While your boyfriend or hubbie is having his fun around the back, grab a vibrator and have some fun up front. Your orgasms will help cover up any painful sensation you might feel and provide both of you with a wild ride! Additional distractions include:

   a) Watching porn of your choice while he is working his way in.

   b) Dirty talk from him to keep your arousal heightened.

   c) Additional props that turn you on: Tying you up, nipple clamps, a video camera, etc.

   d) Oral-Anal Play – There are several flavored anal lubes that can assist with this extremely hot and fun time together. Once you have cleaned for hygiene purposes, ask your partner to lube you up and lick a little back off of you. That will bring you pleasurable sensations before he enters you, hence continuing the relaxation suggestions we made above. After he eats you out from behind, grab your vibrator and continue with your own pleasure as you will be so turned on in that moment that any pain you may experience just might be a little pain with your game that you completely enjoy.

e) Position – Different body types require different positions to maximize comfort. You might want to bend over something, or lie flat on your stomach while you are being entered from behind. Lying on your back and allowing him to work his way in might allow for a more relaxing and intimate experience. Another option is for you to be on top. This way you have total control and you can decide how quickly and how far his penis can enter you for the entire act. If you decide to try the top option, he can lie on his back, or sit in a chair, whichever position is easiest for you to maneuver your bottom.

If he is sitting upright, he can help you with your balance by supporting you while you work out your comfort level with the rate of insertion. Another option is for you to lay on your side and have him spoon you as he works his way in so that you are relaxed and comfortable and he does all the work!

Tripp's Tips:

If you are on top, you are in control, if you lie on your back, he will go much deeper, and if you lie on your side, you can relax and adjust your legs to make yourself most comfortable. Now, here is the thing, his favorite position will probably be doggie style, which most people find the most comfortable position for newbies. It allows both of you to work together to determine rhythm. If you want to really rock his world, bury your chest in the bed, arch your back, and fix your cute ass in a set place. He will do all the work and you will experience more pleasure.

5) Speaking of control – If you need to stop at any time, you stop. Set up a safety word or let your partner know beforehand you might need to tell him it's not going to happen that time. Put in place whatever communication piece needs to occur before the act to ensure that you are protected if you need a little more time and space to make this a successful act for you both.

Tripps Tips:

Establish a safety word. My suggestion: "Bottoms Down!"

Q8: "What About Pleasing Him Anally?"

What's good for the goose is good for the gander, except the gander in this story will have a huge orgasm if he decides he wants to swap positions. The anal vibrators you purchased to help loosen you up will be perfect to explore his rectum in search of his prostate, as long as you thoroughly clean them first. As for finding his prostate, let me tell you ladies, it is not half as elusive as our G-spot. As stated earlier, the end of his prostate is located about three inches inside of his anal cavity. Once you find it, you can move your finger gently back and forth, giving your man more pleasure than he has ever felt before. There are several things you can do while pleasing him anally, but you will have to read the next Tripp N' Allie guidebook to find out!

Tripp's Tips:

As Allie said, make sure you have thoroughly cleansed the anal vibrators he used on you if you are going to use them on him. Hygiene is the key to anal sex! Hopefully, he has his own set of vibrators waiting for you to play. Oh, and one more thing, here is what you do now to get him begging for a deeper experience. You know that wonderful area between his anus and his testicle.

It is actually the hidden gateway to a man and anal sex. But more about that in "Bottom's Up 2 – His Bottom is Up, Too!"

Q9: "What If I Just Can't Do It?"

Stop right there – no one is telling you that anal is mandatory. If you are the little train that couldn't, you gave it a good try! As we stated at the end of question 5, your boundaries must be respected. If it's quittin' time, be open and honest and ask that this activity cease. If anal sex is not something you are physically or emotionally comfortable with, then you need to release yourself to explore many other wonderful, sensual, intimate experiences with your partner. You honored his request by trying and, if you are not successful, there are plenty of other fun, sexy, wild, and hot fantasies for the two of you to act out and find mutual pleasure with each other. He loves you and no doubt feels validated and cared about that you attempted his request. He will love it if you bring alternate suggestions to the table to keep your sex life exciting.

Tripp's Tips:

If anal is not in the cards, my tip is to keep a look out for more Tripp N' Allie guidebooks and try something else in the bedroom – or kitchen, living room, shower, car...

Conclusion:

You did it! Or you are about to! If you have completed this book the you are ready to take on anal. You got this, girl, and your partner is going to be thrilled, in several ways. We are proud of you – you came, you saw, and as soon as your partner orgasms due to anal intercourse, girlfriend, you CONQUERED!

And there's more! You've heard of the Mile High Club? Well, my friend, you are going to be inducted into the Outback Club. You might not have sealed the deal in a jumbo jet, but once your man has entered in what used to be the no-fly zone, your accent will sound as Aussie as Crocodile Dundee. Well, your accent probably won't change, but your sexual status will. And to maintain your membership, make sure you continue to use your anal vibrators on a regular basis, either during vaginal intercourse or while masturbating, to keep those muscles prepared for anal sex. Be sure to check out the rest of the Trip N' Allie Guidebooks as they are released in your area!